EMBRACING THE BATTLE

Tried by Fire

Stories Compiled By

NICOLE JONES

Copyright 2021 Nicole Jones

All rights reserved. In accordance with U.S. Copyright Act of 1976, the scanning, uploading, and electronic sharing of any part of this book without permission of the author is unlawful piracy and theft of the author's intellectual property.

If you would like to use material from the book other than for review purposes, prior permission must be obtained by contacting Nicole Jones.

The Writer's
BLOCK

Contents

Introduction 1

1. On My Own 3
2. Beautifully Broken: Rebuilding Me Piece by Piece 9
3. "The Impact of Triple AAA" 15
4. I Couldn't Take Another Breath, BUT God 21
5. The Day the Emotional Levees Broke 27
6. When Life Changed…. 33
7. Come out Alive 39
8. Porn, A Marital Infidelity 45
9. Strength Found by the Fire 51
10. A Beautiful Lyric 57
11. I'm Still Here 63
12. What's Love Got to do with it? 69
13. Whoosah, It's Okay 75
14. A Letter to My 15-year-old Self 81
15. Please Don't Judge Me 87
16. Changing My Focus from Man to God 93
17. Second Wind, My Story Is Changing: 99

Introduction

Everyone has residue from the ugly parts of their lives, emotionally, sometimes financially, physically, and even socially. We'll call them ashes. Long after you've moved past the situation, there are ashes. Let's face it; we all have been wounded and scarred by battles. We think to ourselves, "If I cover up this wound quickly, I won't feel so exposed."

This book is a collection of true, raw, real-life stories of situations that literally felt like fiery trials. The women in this book endured the flames of disappointment, shame, guilt and fear, yet came out shining as pure gold. In these stories, you will read about how they all had to **stop** responding in fear, **drop** to their knees in prayer, and **roll** under the smoke as it rose above them.

Being tried by fire is defined as "a test of someone's abilities to perform well under pressure," and the co-authors of "Embracing the Battle" know all too well what it is like to walk through fiery trials and to be tried on every hand. When you are determined that NOTHING can stop you, not even fire, you find a way to push ahead and fight through! You could literally be placed in a furnace of life and come out without even a stench of smoke. It is then that you come to respect the power of being ***TRIED BY FIRE***.

• CHAPTER 1 •

On My Own

As a little girl, I can't remember if I had dreams of becoming a mommy or not, like most girls. But what I know is whatever I imagined motherhood to be, I didn't think I would do it alone. I wasn't a teenager. I was a 30-year-older woman riding home in the back seat of my mother's car with a 3-day-old baby in tow. It was a cold and dreary day. It looked like snow was coming soon.

As we sat at the last red light before turning onto my street, I remember saying, "Lord, please let me be able to take care of my baby. Please let me be able to take care of her by myself." My grandmother taught me to be strong, take care of my business, and never ask anyone for anything. As I continued my prayer, I asked God to please let my grandmother live long enough that my child would know and remember her. I wanted her to grow up with the same love in her heart that I had in mine. I wanted her to have the opportunity to learn from my grandmother, just as I had.

A few minutes later, we pulled into my driveway. My mother settled us in, but she had to leave. And then this thing happened... I felt like I was in the world alone, and emotionally I couldn't do it. I felt cold, and I was scared. I laid on the bed with my newborn next to me, and wept. I was almost afraid to touch her. Just as postpartum depression began to sneak up on me, my aunt answered my call, and with tears rolling down, I said, "I can't do this. I can't be here alone." It was within what felt like only a few minutes, she knocked at my door, and I have been leaning on her ever since.

Fast forward a few years, the same relationship that gave me my first blessing birthed another. I was happy, excited, sad, frustrated, and lost all at the same time. People questioned my decisions, and I'm sure they talked behind my back. The question "When are you all getting married?" was just as frequent as "How are you doing?" Sometimes I felt ashamed. Here I was, an educator, never married with two kids. I was supposed to be the positive influence and role model, but my package didn't look like the storybook we are supposed to follow.

Other times, I didn't care because my focus was on being a mommy of two. But on the inside, I never seemed to stop hurting. Doing this thing called parenthood practically alone was tough. I cried many days and nights longing for a missing piece but most of all still praying to God that I could do it BY MYSELF. I looked strong on the outside. The pain was masked with play dates and late nights of hard work. Living on my one salary may be more than what some people have, but it was minimal for me. There were days when I cried because I needed to "rob Peter to pay Paul."

Other days, I cried because I wanted to do simple things that others take for granted. There were also days when having a family unit would have just looked better, and that hurt too. Not only were there things that I couldn't provide because of insufficient resources, but there were also the problems of co-parenting that were problematic and sometimes troubling. Yes, I could have asked for help, but my pride wouldn't allow me to do so. Sometimes, I wonder if that was me being strong or me being too scared of rejection. Whatever it was, in some ways, it held me in bondage. Because of this, I put all my efforts into being mommy, team mom, classroom mom, and any other mom that in my mind meant I was doing what was right for my two.

Sometimes I think that my path is a result of growing up fatherless, being born to a teenage mother, and being raised by my grandmother. I am who I am as a result of my childhood (good and bad). Maybe I have been longing for some missing part from my childhood. Maybe I looked for love in the wrong places, or maybe the type of parent I am is because of my subconscious desire to prove that I am enough. Whatever it is, it has made me stronger.

Yes, this battle has been hard. It almost took me out, but I thank God for His mercy and grace that have given me the power to rise above in so many ways. Thank God for the people He has placed in my life. I have learned a lot from my village, my experiences, and even from my pain. Being a single mother has been the blessing that allows me to love my children even more. They are my why, and it is because of them I have pushed myself through four degrees and now entrepreneurship. My love for them and desire to be an example to them has allowed me to become open to love and companionship again, something I have been battling with. I am blessed to have made through the fire emotionally and physically.

Do I have it all figured out? No. Is life now a bed of roses? No. But I know God heard my cry on many nights. I know that when I thought He had left me; He was only making me stronger by pushing me through experiences that would allow me to understand my purpose. That drive home in late December with a newborn was the beginning of strength like no other. It's no longer about not having a second half, but more about making what I have equal to 100% of enough.

Demetrice Jennings is an Educational Leader within the public-school setting. She is an entrepreneur specializing in real estate and consumer credit. Demetrice uses her acquired skills in teaching and learning to build trustworthy relationships in her business. She serves her community by being a servant and charismatic leader who encourages unity and high standards in everyone. She has successfully helped many families reach their goals and dreams. Demetrice is a lifelong learner with degrees from Florida A&M University, Mercer University, and Valdosta State University.

Demetrice is a proud mother of a young adult daughter and teenage son. Her passion in life is heightened by the growth of her children. Demetrice was born the oldest child and grandchild. She prides herself on being raised by her mother, grandparents, and aunts/uncles. Her family village's strength has inspired her to be a part of this unique anthology.

• CHAPTER 2 •

Beautifully Broken: Rebuilding Me Piece by Piece

I know by now all the chapters are sounding the same. I totally understand how you feel, but see, this isn't that. I'm not your average chick, and neither is my story. Who am I? Let's start with the basics. I was born in the summer of the '80s. I come from a huge family. I had my mom, my grandfather, and my dad. I have known my grandfather and dad my whole life. My grandmother raised me from the age of two until about fourteen years old. I was brilliant in school and was brought up in the AME church. I'm talking about three services a day—every choir rehearsal and Bible study.

On top of that, my grandmother was Rev. Harper, later Rev. Brown., St. Mark's special praise and worship leader until she died. Doesn't sound that bad, right? Ooh chile, you don't know the half. Let me tell you, I'm crazy and a little thrown off, but here are my top five issues: abandonment, trust, addiction, abuse, and expectations. Not in any order, but the biggest influences on my everyday life. No matter how long ago, you never forget. So, let me sum up all these right quick.

Abandonment:
My mother would call and say that she was coming to get me, and two times out of ten she did.

Trust:
I was molested by a family member. The sad part about it is, I didn't know it was wrong. I pretended to be asleep so maybe it would be like a nightmare that I could forget.

Addiction:
My parents battled their demons with drugs and alcohol. I raised my siblings the best I could, starting at the age of 14. They had what they needed to survive, even if I didn't. I don't regret this because the state would have had us, but they weren't taking my babies away from me. I love them

to death. And with mom being gone, I needed them even more.

Abuse:
They say that abuse is a cycle that repeats, and I know it's true for a few reasons but let me tell you, I broke the cycle so that my daughters would never see that or become a victim and think it's normal. Even when the bruises heal, the mental is still damaged.

Expectations:
This last one is all on me. My grandmother mapped out my life long before I could have a choice in the matter, and my father was the same way. I didn't live up to their standards. As soon as I made my choices, the disappointment was evident initially, but one person didn't care what I did as long as I gave it my all and succeeded in it. (my grandfather's expectations)

I have slept in places that you will never catch me in again. I've lived in people's basements and slept on couches as well. I've been hungry and been stuck between a rock and a hard place, betrayed by friends and family. At one point, I walked with my head down and bowed. I would never make eye contact. But with all these obstacles, one thing that I have never done is give up, and my kids have never been hungry. I have let people treat me the way they wanted. They talked down on me, and at one point, I believed them. I didn't speak up for myself.

I didn't want to tell you many of these things, and honestly, if a friend of mine didn't remind me that someone may need to hear this, it'd be going to the grave. I have plenty of failed relationships, multiple baby daddies, and plenty of kids. But I got someone to love me enough to marry me, even though he might regret it now lol. I deserve it and so do you. I'm not going to lie to you. I've had my battles with depression, low self-esteem, and not-so-happy-thoughts. I believed that I didn't deserve the love that I received from my husband and my kids. My two youngest girls are always telling me that I'm the best and that they love me. To them, I am, but as for me, I think they could do better. I'm nowhere near the person they see. I find myself telling them that I'm not, but that's something that I'm working on—learning how to accept a compliment.

All my kids love me unconditionally, and I'm trying to get there for myself. I'm still a work in progress. I've been through more than the average, and different parts of my life have broken me, but that's the key. Once you realize your worth and see yourself through the eyes of the ones who love you most, you can handle anything. I accept that

I'm "Beautifully Broken" and rebuilding myself piece by piece. I know that God's not done with me yet. I am Holy enough to pray with you yet hood enough to swing on you. You see, I know how to speak in tongues, but also can knuck if you buck. You never know what you may get messing with me.

To my family and friends that have had to deal with my crazy self, I'm sorry (not). But in all seriousness, please keep pushing, no matter how long it may take you. When they break you down, pick up the pieces and put yourself back together again.

Lernae Gulley is a mother of nine, wife, sister, and aunt. She wears many hats and rocks them all very well.

Email: lernaegulley@gmail.com
Facebook: Lernae Childs Gulley
P.O. Box 414 Morrow, Ga 30260

• CHAPTER 3 •

"The Impact of Triple AAA"

"You're an amazing woman," is the phrase I've heard time and time again. Those words were often said after the "words." The words scar. The words attempt to tear you down. The threats get louder in your mind and cause you to second guess who you are. The words tribble the beat of your heart, and they diminish the pace of your steps—words formed as threats. Words formed to pierce your heart, causing you to bleed out silently, screaming for help. The words are painful.

Words are our primary form of communication and are not meant to hurt. I once read that words can "send a bolt of emotional distress straight through an individual's heart and soul." This has been my experience. Verbally abused by those who I felt were closest to me, those whom I allowed to penetrate my seven-layer protective bubble and get close enough to me to cut me with their words.

In my marriage, I was a helper. If I described myself with one word, it would be anticipator. I am an anticipator of needs. I used to pride myself on always filling in the gap and anticipating the next steps. What else needs to be done, where can I fix the issue, and how can I make this better? That was the pattern of my relationships in my marriage, childhood, and everyday life.

After a few years of marriage, I was met daily with demands and conquest that would require me to submit to actions I disagreed with, and once those disagreements surfaced, I was met with an array of phrases that cut to the core.

"You're not good enough for me."
"You're lying to me."
"You need to do what I am telling you to do."

These were all triggers for me and have caused a large amount of anger that grew larger and larger day after day. As an only child raised in a military-style household, I was used to straight, direct instructions but never was I met with criticism that was disguised as love. How can words from a person you love cause you so much pain? Fighting the feelings, you continue to pursue the love you think you need, even if it is caused by someone you love.

You fight the embarrassment of broadcasting the tear downs, and you place a smile on your face day after day. You keep moving while hurting in silence. Internalization is how most victims of verbal abuse hide the fact that they're being abused. These feelings typically lead to thoughts of fear, insignificance, untrusting, emotionally needy, and unlovable. You begin to question why you feel so bad, and you can't understand why it is happening to you.

All abuse is not physical abuse. Enduring verbal threats and demanding tactics day in and day out is mentally, physically, and emotionally exhausting, and for four years of my life, that is what I endured. Being chained to "the words" is exhausting. It drains you, and you must continue to live life through the fatigue. In my almost 41 years, I have learned to combat the mental and physical paralysis of being a verbal abuse victim. This overcoming journey cannot be made alone, and one must be honest about its impact on your life. Here are a few steps that I have taken to remember who I am both in trying times.

The Three A's

1. **Acknowledge** the emotional distress that you're experiencing. You will be unable to heal what you will not acknowledge. This was the hardest part of my journey because I was in denial about accepting that someone I loved, would hurt me. Admit that you've been hurt and accept the healing journal which is ahead.

2. **Affirm** to yourself verbally every day that you are above the criticism and the critical conditions used to tear you down. Affirmations are used to reprogram your mind and to encourage you to believe positive things about yourself. I mastered the power of affirmation a few years before my divorce and still plaster the mirrors around my home with positive statements.
Examples: No one can hurt you or make you feel inferior without your permission.
Beauty begins the moment you decide to meet yourself.

Affirmations help you by adjusting long-standing beliefs that have hindered your ability to move forward, and they will strengthen your confidence by reminding you of who you are!

3. **<u>Align</u>** yourself to a renewed purpose, and do not allow anything to prevent you from seeing it come to pass. During my separation, I devoted my time to reintroduce myself to the world but first, by re-introducing myself to ME! The alignment will require you to let go of control and allow things to flow with purpose. Visualize your goals, write them down and do whatever it takes to make them happen. You must align your daily actions – your life, with your goals.

Renewing my vision on the power of words has caused me to create a motto for my life – "the process never looks like the end results." You may have gone through a season of verbal and emotional abuse – that is not your result. You may have had to retrain your mind to put yourself first – that is not your end result. Love yourself again, protect your heart and remember the three A's – acknowledge the abuse, affirm yourself, and align with your renewed purpose.

LeNora is an affirmer, dreamer, friend, soror, curator, and giver. She has been living in the Atlanta Metropolitan area for over 20 years, and as such, has coined herself an "Adopted Peach." Serving the judiciary by day and her community all other hours, LeNora is a present help to all of those in need. Whether it's volunteering with the March of Dimes or serving as a board member to numerous public and civic organizations, LeNora's nurturing spirit is always at work. An altruist, she is always willing to give in ways that stretch her imagination.

Constantly cultivating the skills garnered in her master's and graduate certification programs, LeNora looks eagerly ahead to what she will offer others in the decades to come. Always remembering and living by the quote coined by Dana Cunningham, Ph.D. that "If it doesn't bring me peace, it's not worth it," LeNora always strives to protect her peace by any means necessary.

• CHAPTER 4 •

I Couldn't Take Another Breath, BUT God

How do I allow myself to go back to this place, a place of hurt and pain? My prayer is that I will encourage someone. When you feel like you cannot take another breath, you can. Know God is right there with you, carrying you and understanding every moan and acknowledging every tear.

Sinking…

The pain never fully goes away, it is just something you learn to deal with. As soon as I think about the event, my cells have an amazing way of allowing me to recall. The body can conceal what the heart has a hard time dealing with and even rationalizing. I found myself four months pregnant, being rushed to the emergency room trying to save my baby. As nurses poked me, I was numb. Numb with confusion and fear. Fear of the unknown and confused about what this meant for me. Once the doctor (who will remain nameless) told us to abort, we had to decide. Should we go with the doctor or God? We chose God. We were raised to put all hope, faith, and trust in God AND pray for a miracle.

As I laid in the bed with the lower portion of my body elevated, there were moments of extremes. The highs were the days when nurses would come and weigh me. They would say everything looked good. Those times made me feel encouraged and motivated. Low days were when the doctor would tell us to, "Give up, go ahead and get rid of it so you guys can move on." I would look at him with disgust. I told him he would not make the decision. My husband and I would shake our heads "NO" and continue to fight another day. We hugged, held hands, cried, and prayed.

People came to visit. Our family and friends were distractors. Their presence provided a break from the mental turmoil. They brought food, smiles, and laughter. People prayed over me, the baby, and Dax, while we held on to hope. I looked for scriptures in the Bible to read. I was grasping, wanting to make this make sense. There were days I felt lonely, mostly days when Dax would go to work. The minutes felt like hours, and the days seemed endless. I found myself looking for bright spots.

One day that stands out is when the doctor came and told us that there was nothing he could do if I went into labor five months pregnant. I would have to deliver, but once the cord was cut, that would be the end of the baby's life. Should we continue or give up? After Dax and I prayed, we decided to keep fighting. WE felt like we could not give up. Then early one morning, I woke up, and things did not feel right. I woke Dax up and told him to get a nurse. The nurse came in and told us I was in labor. I was a few days from being five months pregnant. Hours later, the doctor arrived and said, "I told you!" His chilly disposition was what I expected. The labor progressed, and the pain intensified. The physical pain of labor and mental pain knowing what awaited us.

As the hours passed, they gave me something for the pain, but there was nothing they could give me for my heart. I knew what was bound to happen. As Dax hurried and called our parents, I could see he was breaking even in my pain. His voice cracked, and tears rolled from his eyes as labor continued. Once she was born, I knew it was already over. It was done before it started. The doctor cut the cord, and her life ended. At that point, had to figure out who I was.

I do remember being able to see her dressed. We named her Kyndal Faith. There she was, beautiful and lifeless. She was a precious combination of Dax and me. I held her then I yelled, screamed, and cried. I broke…. Everything in and on my body hurt. Who was I? Once I was released from the hospital, I found myself weak physically, emotionally, and spiritually. I didn't want to be here. I was done.

I felt like God had let me down. My prayer life stopped, but I thank God for those who prayed for me. Each day seemed like the day before. I was lost. When people called and quoted the Bible, I would hang up. I was not interested at all. Then one day, I woke up and said, "Thank you, God." That was all I had, but at least it was a start. I remember having a gathering at my house a month after Kyndal passed. After everyone left, I wept. How dare I have a good time, and she was not here. What did I have to smile about? My emotions were scrambled, and I couldn't find a reason to dismiss the claim. There were highs and lows coupled with tears and laughter, all in rapid succession.

Then shame set in and I felt limited. The thought of returning to work was overwhelming. I had to face it my new reality. Was I going to shrink away or heal? Healing is tough, but I decided to heal. What I understand now is there are only two emotions, love and fear. Everything positive comes from love, and everything negative comes from fear. So, where did my shame come from? It came from a place of fear, but what was I afraid of? I was afraid that I was not measuring up to the standard of being a woman. Giving birth is something that should happen easily, and for me, in this instance, I could not do it. Whose standard was I not measuring up to? Even deeper, who created the standard? The disappointment was another emotion I had to deal with. I was afraid I had let my husband down. Will he look at me differently? Will he still find me attractive? Will he feel like I let him down because I could not complete this mission? Once I faced it and healed, it became easier to take a breath and breathe.

Angela T. Benton is a speaker, teacher, and entrepreneur who used life's experiences to gain a wealth of knowledge. She has learned how to inspire people to heal and honor themselves, so they can ultimately soar.

By leaning on her life's passion for teaching, she has learned how to reach a wide range of people. After writing a self-help book for parents about how to navigate through education, she found it necessary to extend her hand by leveling with people and sharing an inner portion of herself. Angela lives by her quote of "Learning how to move through hurt, pain, and trauma by healing your heart and finding your voice." With a knack for listening without judging, Angela has been able to minister to many as they travel through their personal life's path.

• CHAPTER 5 •

The Day the Emotional Levees Broke

The funeral is a blur for me. I recall being at home after the burial, surrounded by a flurry of family. I was numb and in shock but was completely unaware of these feelings in the moment. My childhood friend asked if I wanted to hang out with her family away from my home. I asked my mom for her permission, and she obliged. I was a 13-year-old kid who just participated in the funeral for my father, and I couldn't remember what happened. All I knew was I needed to get away. Denial sat in my body and mind, but I was determined to stay there for as long as I could; forever was the intention.

I've heard so many people share the experience of being by their loved one's bedside, holding their hands, sharing the last moments, and saying their final goodbyes when terminal illness sets in. Well, that wasn't my story.

I recall a hospital bed fixed in the living room of our home. My mom and two older sisters watched cancer take the life out of daddy. When I saw that hospital bed in my house, I can't even tell you what I felt. It's still hazy today, 27 years later.

My daddy was chocolate, sported a fro until the day he passed (although I asked him for years to trim his hair), had the brightest smile, and was a man's man. He was about 6 feet tall, walking into rooms like a "Warrior." Daddy perfectly personified our surname. As a little girl, I remember tipping into the bathroom to watch him shave his face. I would stand on top of the closed commode, leaning into the sink as he applied the shaving cream. I stood there as a small child in awe of her daddy. I was his baby girl; Pooh is what he called me. I just knew my daddy was a superhero and he could do anything in my eyes.

One day, daddy was moving out of the living room into the hospital. Shortly after, his home was in a hospice facility. The following Friday, my oldest sister told me she would pick me up from school that day to see daddy. I was 13, so there was so much my mom and sisters shielded me from. I completely get it now; they didn't want to endure the pain of the details. My ignorance did not allow me to recognize this type of facility specialized in providing comfortable spaces for terminally ill patients.

On this particular Friday, I was distracted at school because my thoughts were on daddy. I planned to have a specific conversation with him. I didn't verbalize this to anyone because I wanted the moment to be between him and me. His baby girl had some things to say to her superhero. The end of the school day is here, and my big sister picks me up as we head home before going to see daddy. When we walked into the house, my sister's boyfriend was standing in the kitchen. My mom and other sister were standing there as well. Silence and a spooky spirit were in the room. The light was off, and I knew he was gone. My heart sank and shattered. I was a fatherless child. I was shoved into being numb, angry, and in denial. And I immediately put my mask of "everything will be okay" on my face and in my heart.

For nearly seven years, I wore my mask of denial and protection. From birth, I've been a ball of energy and optimism. My childhood was one of running, skipping, writing, dancing, singing, reading, talking, and seeing life as a beautiful and magical place full of possibilities and imagination! This is who I was and still am. Once my daddy passed, I stayed right there. I didn't grieve, and I didn't know how to. Although I am the youngest of three, I certainly wasn't going to fill the rooms I entered with sadness and dreary emotions. I clicked on the switch of survival and didn't turn it off.

I matriculated through school as an honor student and received a full academic scholarship to THE Alabama A&M University in Huntsville, AL. At 18, I knew I couldn't stay in Georgia. I was over my sweet momma's old school rules and needed to fly my way. So, I went there and had the time of my life. I formulated so many healthy friendships and learned layers of lessons on "The Hill." Leaving home at that time was necessary for me as I began to understand who Brandy was. By this time, I was in love with Jesus. No more was He my momma's best friend, but Jesus was also mine.

I was in my dorm suite one day by myself. I was sitting on my bed, wearing black shorts and a black tank top. Something stirred in me that caused me to take that invisible mask off. Someone was praying for me now that I think about it. Someone knew I needed release. I cried like I've never cried before about my daddy. I cried until I had no tears left to give. I finally allowed the wall I built for years to crack. I released the hurt, anger, and sadness. I finally felt the aching inside my heart, the void my dad left there. I finally forgave him for leaving me without having our final conversation. I forgave myself for holding on to this for years.

God placed a spiritual blanket of healing across my back and gave me the physical space to release without interruptions from anyone. My phone didn't ring, and no one entered the suite; it was just me, God, and my daddy in that room. That was the beginning of a new day for me. That day, the mask began to break. I didn't know there were additional steps I had to take to destroy the mask. But the breakthrough process of freedom began...

Brandy is an Atlanta native, daughter of Mrs. Rudene H. Warrior and the late Willie R. Warrior. She fell in love with writing as a child, constantly journaling her thoughts and dreams. Her attraction to reading, writing, music, and dance framed Brandy's personality as a creative and joyous kid.

Always living to the beat of her drum, Brandy is a proud Black woman, writer, speaker, healer, and avid seeker of self-improvement. She relies heavily on the Holy Spirit, her ancestors, and therapy to guide her. Brandy is a divorced mommy of a brilliant and loving young king, Antonio, and a member of Delta Sigma Theta Sorority, Inc. She is a confidant, friend, lover of life, old soul, encourager, positive person, and prayer warrior. Her prayer is that God's light will shine through her as she intentionally lives a balanced life to the beat of an 80's R&B soundtrack.

IG: buttafly_bran
FB: Brandy Manning (Warrior)
YouTube: Brandy Warrior

• CHAPTER 6 •

When Life Changed...

I moved to Atlanta in the early '90s, as many considered it as the "Land of Milk and Honey." If you can't make it here, then face the possibility that you can't make it at all. I went through the ups and downs. I married and thought that I needed to go with the flow, and eventually, life would slow down. Well, guess what, it didn't! I CONSTANTLY lived under an extreme amount of stress.

After my youngest child's graduation exercises, many older relatives were transitioning from life on this side and dealing with stress from work. FINALLY, I decided to divorce my cheating spouse. After which, I had a major milestone birthday on the horizon. THE BIG 50!! So, I threw a Golden 50 Party. I also decided to get my 1st passport stamp and visit Jamaica!

The following year I began to experience light headiness, frequent headaches, and strange smells. I observed that I always seemed to drop light-weighted items when that was never a problem before. My memory began to fail me. I ignored all those medical signs or conveniently explained them away. So, I decided to throw myself another party to celebrate year 51. As the week was leading up, I experienced the same cognitive abnormalities, but I constantly explained them away. On my birthday, I went to work as usual, attended choir rehearsal, and met a few friends for dinner.

Looking back now, I didn't feel like myself but explained it away. Awakening Friday morning, I started to prepare for work but could not shake a voice clearly speaking to me saying, "DO NOT DRIVE TO WORK. IT IS NOT SAFE." This happened not once but several times. I then decided not to go to work, and I found myself incredibly sleepy. I thought I just needed rest, or if I had eaten something that did not agree with me. I needed ginger-ale! I got in my car, went to the gas station, went inside, got the ginger-ale out of cooler, and could barely stand.

The store employees looked at me strangely, but I shrugged it off. I got back in my car and drove home. I pulled into the driveway and ended up hitting the garage door. As soon as I turned off the engine, my son came outside and calmly stated that I hit the garage and he needed my keys because I could NOT drive. He then assisted me to my room, took my keys, and that was the last time I saw them until I was released from the hospital. After falling asleep again, I couldn't understand why I could not stay awake. A friend had tickets for an engagement at City Winery, but I had fallen asleep midday and failed to contact my employer. This was NOT like me!!! "What is going on?! It is clear something is not right. Did someone slip me a mickey?!" So many questions, but no answers.

When I awakened Saturday morning, the "dropsies" returned. While feeding my pooch, I dropped an entire bag of dog food all over the kitchen. My son came downstairs to investigate the ruckus, only to find me inappropriately dressed. "Ma, what are you doing?" he asked, as I stood only wearing a bra and pajama bottoms. Something certainly wasn't right. I fell asleep on the couch, then moved upstairs to my bedroom and slept soundly again!! My family became very concerned and made me go to the hospital. They explained that they would feel better once the doctors evaluated my symptoms. I was unable to dress myself and had to have my sister-in-law and my best friend do it for me.

Once arriving at the hospital, the med team determined that my symptoms were more than they could handle, and I would need to be transferred to Emory. I was in tears because I couldn't understand what was going on. I was transported to Emory Hospital on June 3, 2017, and the next time I was fully conscious was June 16, 2017.

I awakened to being told that I had swelling on the brain. They had performed a brain biopsy, multiple MRIs, and CT Scans. The med team diagnosed a rare autoimmune condition, Central Nervous System Vasculitis. I had experienced a flare up and was extremely fortunate to be alive because things were "touch and go" a few times. After spending an additional week within the lofty accommodations at Emory Hospital, that I have quite affectionately renamed to "Club Em," I was released to return home.

My family told me that many people were worried about me and constantly checked on my progress. Returning home was scary. I wasn't released to return to work, and I wasn't sure when/if I could return as the condition typically leaves patients with severe brain fog. How would I take care of myself and my home? I was also my mom's caregiver, so I worried that I wouldn't be able to care for her. Why was this happening to me? What would I do, and how could my family get along? Is this really what my life is resulting to?

Here I was starting to live my best life as the sexy divorcee and empty nester, now facing the possibility of being the "old sickly lady." Immediately I resolved to learn everything about my condition and turn my lemons into lemonade. I reviewed all the test results that had been performed. I read them several hours per day. I checked out the acceptable and below acceptable results. I figured out what I could do to correct my condition, and what behaviors to adapt to maintain and raise the ratings to acceptable levels.

I had been prescribed meds but was curious about the long-term effects. I had to become an advocate for myself. Every visit, I asked questions about things that I had researched. Taking full accountability for my journey and being determined to control the narrative; I joined a support group and have learned even more. There were people there who have had this illness from their teens, to their 60's. The members of the group have taught me many things and they gave me the one thing that I needed the most--HOPE.

Lisa Swann Middlebrooks is an advocate of self-health. Through her own crisis, she learned and always shares the importance of being your OWN BEST advocate. Her entire life changed after been diagnosed with a serious auto-immune condition. Self-education of the life-threatening illness allowed her to extend what was proposed as possibly the end.

This way of behaving was nothing new as she gave birth to one of her children at 6-months gestation and successfully cared for and raised the child to adulthood. Through that experience, she learned the importance of health advocacy. She is available to partner with individuals experiencing health care challenges.

She focuses on steps that should be next in health care advocacy to improve the lives/outlook for patients or loved ones with health challenges and improving the relationship between patients and their families with strategic medical partnerships. She can be reached at lymbrooks66@gmail.com.

CHAPTER 7

"Come out Alive"

The year was 2007. The kids were eight, five, and four. We were living in Maryland, and my husband at the time was deployed overseas. My routine was to pick the kids up from school, come home and fix dinner, watch a little tv, then baths and bed. This night, I'd thrown a load of clothes in the washer and put them in the dryer before going to bed. I'd done that so many times before that I never even thought about it.

I can sleep pretty hard at times, but this night was different. At 1:05 am (I can literally still see the bright red numbers from the clock on the nightstand), I was awakened by a sound, a cracking sound. As the sound became clearer, I sat up and put my feet out of bed. At that moment, the smoke detectors in the house started blaring at the same time my feet hit the carpet. That's when I knew our house was on FIRE!

On a cold Maryland night, at 1:00 in the morning, my house was on fire and the children were asleep in their rooms. I didn't even know where the fire was, but I knew that we needed to get out of the house IMMEDIATELY! I calmly but quickly walked down the hall to Jeremy's room first because it was the farthest away. My heart was racing, but I had to stay calm, or I'd scare the kids. The sound of every smoke detector going off was deafening. I went to Nicholas' room to wake him and across the hall to Kennedy.

The kids were scared, but they trusted the calmness and assurance in my eyes that we'd all be okay if they just did what I said. Just this time, listen exactly to what mommy says and do exactly what she said. This was not the time for questions. It was time to move quickly. We got downstairs and each time we moved another step without being confronted with flames, I thanked God. I remember saying "Thank You Jesus" repeatedly. We hopped in my truck, pulled out of the garage, and I called 911.

"911, what's your emergency?"

"I believe my house is on fire."

The operator asked me if I saw any flames. I was like, "Did I see any flames? I wasn't looking for any!" I told her to send the fire department immediately.

By this time, my neighbor across the street heard the fire alarms and took the kids out of the cold. She tried to calm them down as she could see fear and worry in their eyes. She assured them that they were okay. I am forever grateful for Winona Lee & her grandmother, Gi Gi. They were angels to us so many times.

After a few minutes, I heard the sirens. The fire engine whipped around the corner and I got out of the car, meeting the firemen in the yard. I explained what little I knew, and they went in to check things out. The next thing I knew, they ran back out and started unwinding the long, thick yellow water hose. No one said anything to me as I stood there bewildered at the fact that I never even knew where the fire was in the house! They went right to work.

It seemed like forever, and so many things went through my mind. What would be destroyed? How would I recover after this? Over that year, we'd endured so much. From the car accident that totaled our other truck, to Jeremy's brain injury, we were constantly being tried. The ironic part is that with every trial, my faith was becoming stronger and stronger.

As time passed, more fire trucks came. One of my neighbors ended up talking to one of the firemen and asked what type of night they'd had. He told her that we were their third house fire that night. She asked what happened with the other two, and we learned that the first house had burned to the ground. In the second fire, there was a fatality. Thirdly, there was our house. The house where there was a fire, but no visible flames. My neighbor was a woman of faith as well, and I remember her looking at me with this astonished look on her face. We both knew! We'd been kept! My children and I had been in a fiery furnace, yet never saw one flame!

Eventually, the lead fireman walked over to me with a piece of burnt equipment in his hand. He told me that the dryer's regulator had malfunctioned, causing the dryer not to shut itself off. It overheated and caught on fire. He told me it was a leading cause of house fires, not lint trays. Even in emptying them, regulators could still overheat. I asked where the fire was, and he told me how lucky we'd been. The fire stayed in the laundry closet in the wall between the laundry closet and Nicholas' room. The fire burned upward and not outward!

Nicholas's bed was on the laundry room wall, so had the fire burned outward, it would have hit his room first. God kept him! The fire stayed in the wall and went up through the roof!! My neighbor called us "the Hebrew children!" She said, "Y'all are some blessed people! You and your children walked right by the fire and don't even smell like smoke!"

When you're in a trial, a fiery trial, all you know is that you have to get out. You can't waste time rationalizing. You can't waste time trying to figure things out, and you can't even waste time looking for flames. You have to come out alive; THAT is your only focus! Coming out alive, unharmed, unscathed, not even smelling like the smoke of the fire you're going through in life. All you know is that you will come out ALIVE!

NICOLE JONES

Nicole Jones is a creative and Kingdom-centered Influencer who embodies crazy, supernatural faith in every aspect of her life. Nicole's down-to-earth yet practical and direct delivery reaches people at their core, yielding transformation and healing in everyone she encounters.

Nicole understands what it is to be stuck, frustrated, and disappointed. She inspires and empowers others to do the same leveraging spirit and truth to bring transformative healing into the world! In her heart is a desire for everyone to win fueled by love and compassion. Nicole uses her own truth, spiritual growth, and self-awareness to empower others to evolve and become the most-highest form of themselves so they too, can impact the world. Nicole is a VP of Human Resources in her professional life, and a mom of three grown children.

CHAPTER 8

Porn, A Marital Infidelity

Oh, how I want to embrace you, have the taste of your lips touch mine and my head lay on your chest with my eyes closed as I count your heartbeats, imagining each one of them for me. Calling your name, yet you do not answer because my lips are sealed. I can hear your laughter and see you watching me, but I turn, and it is a flashback, only a memory.

Where are you? Where are we? How did the sight of you grows dimmer by the day, yet we share the same space and the same last name? Do you remember me? Do you think of me the way you did when we first started? Where is the "you" before I do? I am reaching out, and my voice screams with no sound. I long to feel you, but it is another empty day of silence that yells louder than the noise of the highway in our backyard.

It must be the computer that has your attention again. What are you watching? What has you so captured that it pulls you from me? There was no denying what we felt was real at the start; talks of a future together became a part of our dialogue. Being married before, we wanted to do it right in the sight of God. Sleepovers, before I do, could be counted on one hand. We spent time sharing more of our history, dynamics, goals, truths, and broken places.

Counseling for eight weeks was important to clear the air, teaching us to love one another as we carry residue, not a piece of luggage set into our future. Talks of intimacy and ways we would be sexual with no boundaries to defile our marital bed, thoughts of you and I ran deep. "I do" became "I don't." Don't touch, don't kiss, don't… The distance, coldness, agitation, short words, and little touch began. Nights apart became weeks, and I could tell that something is wrong, very off.

Do I check your phone? Too afraid of what could be, I stared, but my hands could not input the code, afraid of what I would find. Time is going by days, turning into weeks, weeks into an entire month. The words I would hear days later caused me to feel befuddled. There was not another woman but many women, page after page, screen after screen. These were not women on social media where

DMs were slid into. There was no woman for me to confront about my husband. These women lived in the digital world of porn. My husband committed marital infidelity with porn. I almost wanted it to be another woman because that would be real and reachable.

Porn has stepped into my marriage and cooled the bed that was warmed by the love of my husband. I did not understand, and my insecurities began with jealousy of multiple women giving my husband pleasures and attention through digital means at high speeds that should be mine. I thought I was alone, which must not be much of a problem because surely pre-marital counseling would have prepared us for this if it was such a problem. Yet a growing problem it was.

Turning on the television to watch Steve Harvey, a mirror was there, but our voices differed. A couple was mirroring our situation. I saw stories about Kirk Franklin and Pastor Michael Todd. I even shared with a friend and learned that it was true for her household as well. From the famous to church pews, blue and white collars was across marital households of all demographics. From a child to adulthood, I dealt with drug addiction in the life of my parents. Porn, a little peek here and there, no harm right, wrong. Society says it's just sex, right?

My mind was spinning. How did we get here? What didn't I see? Do I leave? How am I to be a helpmeet? This cannot be happening. It is real. This is happening. I cannot fix it and I need help. How many of you can relate? Do not be ashamed to raise your hand; nobody can see you (you're reading a book). Porn addiction is not a personal vendetta against the one feeling offended; it is harder on the offender. Porn addiction brings about guilt, shame, and causes persons to wear a mask and exist, not thriving in the fullness and freedom of authentic living. It is a coping mechanism from trauma, deep-rooted unhealed tragedies, and emotions. Society teaches us it is right to normalize what God never intended. It is more than a sneak peek; it is a catalyst of destruction for the individual and their loved ones.

Is it you, your spouse, or your friend? It does not matter the titles we hold, degrees we earn, if we are in the background or forefront, we all have something. Let us come from hiding into healing by having healthy conversations that will break the chains. My husband seeks consistent counseling to deal with the root of life issues he once covered with porn. He shares his story with many through social media platforms that keep him accountable, reminding others that no one is left to deal with this addiction alone.

Today my fears of porn addiction smothering and choking out my marriage are no longer running rampant with fear. The decision to tell my truth, seek counseling, trust Christ's hand, while keeping mine off, makes it lighter with each passing day. The counselor holds me accountable for taking care of me, not being the fixer, and staying in my lane.

We live in this world but are not subject to take on the norms of this world. Normalizing and stretching boundaries drive a wedge between healing and living healthy. If "everybody" is doing it, then it must be okay. What about standing out and falling in? Telling our truth and seeking help can be the shift that catapults change. No more shame, we will stand together!

Amia Guild, known to many as "Sunshine," a Midwest native from Illinois, born November 05, 1971, is a wife, mother, business owner, and philanthropist. Amia graduated with a bachelor's degree from IUPUI. After years in corporate, she had a greater calling on her life to serve. "If you follow a career not based on money, but in line with the will God has, the money will follow you."

This quote moved Amia from comfort to serving the community, a journey fulfilling purpose. Seeing the need to support our youth, being part of the solution became her launching pad to entrepreneurship as the founder of *"Takes A Village Transportation."* She can serve with a heart's work in communities and families through transportation.

Amia attributes her heart's love for family and community to her anchor in Christ. She enjoys karaoke, family game nights, traveling, volunteering, and hopes for a standup comedy act.

• CHAPTER 9 •

Strength Found by the Fire

Fire altered our lives forever as the parallel of my mother's tragic accident resulted in her search for self, causing me to continuously search for myself. Children evolve into adults based on the environment in which they were raised, their culture, parental involvement, and familial dynamics. I was born in Texas, an only child born to the oldest of five children, by my highly educated mother and grandparents. My grandparents were very loving and nurturing to their children and grandchildren. They instilled in every family member the importance of a quality education and were perfect role models.

However, we all understand that every child is unique and different in their own way. I was the only child born to my eighteen-year-old mother. Raised with my grandparents, I had an uncle, aunts that were three and ten years older than me, and another older aunt and uncle who all were like siblings. At the time, our extended family was extremely close. Our family values provided a sense of stability and comfort. We were a typical close-knit family with all the children and grandchildren staying very close to home.

The day it all fell apart for my stable and loving family would soon cause a domino effect of troubles for each of us individually, and as a family for the rest of our lives. Due to a huge altercation with my uncle, I awaited my mother's arrival to pick me up. That arrival never happened, and as usual, I carried on with my evening. That was really easy to do, as I also had a bedroom at my grandparents' home. My grandparents received a call around 5:00 am the very next morning. This call was from the hospital stating that my mom had been in a serious accident and we would need to get to the hospital right away.

Upon our arrival, my mother was listed as DOA (Dead on Arrival). However, in a miracle that only God could perform, the hospital recanted this belief after my mom lifted her arm as if to say, "I'm still here!" She was only 31 years old with 3rd-degree burns over 80% of her body; and both her legs were amputated on the way to the hospital. My mother was hit from behind by a drunk driver while putting gasoline in her car on the roadside. She was supported by an officer that placed flares around her car to protect and provide a visual barrier.

However, an unlicensed illegal immigrant was too inebriated to heed any applicable warnings. His decision to drive at that very moment completely altered our lives forever. My mother remained in the hospital burn ward for over 365 days. We spent more than half of that time unsure if she would make it out alive. She had over 37 major surgeries to sustain her life and a few to rebuild her completely disfigured body. Doctors explained to my family that we would not recognize my beautiful mother anymore. This information caused me to visit the hospital daily, but I initially refused to enter her room.

Once I was confident and strong enough to prepare for my mother's new appearance, I went to her bedside. We could only enter her room in pairs and fully covered in hospital clothing. No one, not even the doctors, could prepare me for what I was about to witness and the image of my mother that would never leave my mind. Her head was as swollen as a largely pickled watermelon, with crisp black pieces of skin peeling off her naked body. She would lay there with only heat lamps to keep her warm as sheets of fabric would have stuck to her wounds.

There laid my mother, completely unrecognizable, burned, and disfigured by fire. She was a teacher, a mother, a daughter, a friend, a sister, and a young woman with such a promising future, completely altered and changed forever. This dreadful day not only impacted and forever changed her, but it also changed those around her, especially her only child. The next few years were utterly complicated. This accident caused my mother to learn the basics to reinvent herself as a new person, but it also challenged me and our relationship.

It caused her to continuously search for herself in this newly disfigured body as a young woman and mother with reversed roles. As I regularly watched my mother search for herself and cope with her new life, the depression of it all sometimes became unbearable. It was challenging to watch her struggle emotionally, physically, spiritually, and mentally. As she struggled, I struggled too. There wasn't anything I could do to make what she was experiencing better.

My mother died five years after this horrific tragedy; leaving her only daughter at nineteen years old to figure out this thing called life basically all alone. The drunk driver was never found or convicted, and justice never served. I was left with pain, hurt, and brokenness. However, I was also left with experiences and lessons that most would never endure in a lifetime. Losing a parent is never easy. However, appreciating that God could have taken her in the fire, but He gave her life. He granted my mother and me another opportunity to build renewed bonds and a few more years together.

He allowed us to create just a few more precious memories. Her strength and resilience taught me strength and gave me the fire to succeed. Her struggles and journey became my "why." God allowed me to switch from despair to gratefulness. He gave us a few more years together to provide new memories, new norms, and new experiences that I could cherish for the rest of my life. Lessons in darkness teach us to value love and life. I take her strength with me daily as I continuously redefine myself. Continue to love and cherish the opportunity to use your fires to light the fire within.

Melisha Rogers-Harris Ph.D. is a mother, wife, and an educator. She has experienced so many trials and tribulations in life that has truly tested her faith in every aspect. Her down-to-earth attitude and spiritual connectedness allows her never to meet a stranger. She brings love and belonging to everyone she meets.

Melisha understands what it means to lose, love, hurt deeply, and rebuild "self." She uses her leadership background to empower and encourage others to strive, rebuild, and regain themselves. Melisha understands that true healing starts within oneself. However, it takes finding self-love, grit, and the will to succeed to make it happen.

Melisha has traveled the world teaching and learning. She is an education consultant and district leader. Her goal is to help children and adults reach their full potential in all aspects. Dr. Rogers-Harris is married with two biological and two bonus children.

CHAPTER 10

A Beautiful Lyric

Pregnancy is a special time in a mother's life. Though it may be filled with uncertainty, chaos, a little bit of fear and anxiety, it can be one of the best moments in the life of an expectant mother. Finding out I was pregnant for the third time was shocking. I already had two sons, four and two, and I had been getting birth control injections for two years. I must say, finding out that it was a girl made it easier to accept.

During the 7th[th] month, I remember asking my doctor the baby's positioning and recall him telling me that she was head down and feet up, so I asked why I was feeling little sharp kicks that didn't feel like feet? He assured me that it was her feet and I had nothing to worry about; so, on I went, prepping for the arrival of my first princess.

On July 3, 1996, at 7:20 pm, while the fireworks were going off at Navy Pier, Lyric Mariah was born. Immediately after she was born, they wrapped her up and took her out of the room without any explanation. I asked the doctor, the on-call obstetrician, why wasn't I allowed to hold or see my baby, and why did they take her out of the room so fast? He then tried to explain that she had some "webbing" of the fingers and toes on her hands and one of her feet.

I wasn't a nurse at that time, but in my mind, I envisioned the webbing of a duck's feet, so I asked, "Can't that be fixed? Won't she be alright?" I don't even recall what that doctor said from that point as he continued to complete his procedure, and then left out of the room. For the next five hours, I asked to see my baby and was continually told I needed to wait a bit longer. Eventually, I became distraught and walked to the nursery, banging on the window, demanding that I get to see my baby. The sweetest nurse ever opened the door; she looked at me and told me to come on in, as she was just about to bath Lyric, and since I was there, I could do it instead.

She grabbed me by my hand and said, "Now, I want you to be prepared, her hands and feet look a little different, but she is beautiful. So, when you get to her, don't let that take away from this moment, okay?" Not knowing what I was about to see, I just nodded my head in agreement and walked over to the crib. I looked at my little pink and plump baby and noticed she was missing her right foot, and the fingers to both hands were mangled, nothing at all like the doctor described to me. I was just about to start crying when the nurse put her hand on my shoulder and whispered, "Isn't she just the cutest thing? She is strong mama; I can tell by her cry. This one is going to be great; you just watch and see." I caught myself before I even let the first tear fall, and I nodded at the nurse and began giving my baby girl her first bath.

I finally got to speak with my doctor the day after she was born and was told that she was born with Amniotic Band Syndrome. This rare condition causes congenital abnormalities, some even fatal. When the lining of the amniotic sac ruptures or tears, creating bands that form and attach to the fetus' limbs and causes constrictions, essentially cutting off the blood supply, leaving severe congenital disabilities.

Guilt, depression, anger, and even shame began to fill my head, not knowing what I would do. How was I going to be able to raise a child with such needs, and what was I supposed to say to people who asked what happened to her? Are they going to think I was on drugs, or could something that I did cause this? I had no idea how I was going to do this. I remember asking God what I did so bad that He punished my baby.

I dressed her like a baby doll. I even got creative with her booties and stuffed cotton balls into one and used a little hair scrunchy to hold it onto her ankle so that it appeared as though both feet were there. Scratch mittens covered her hands, and I had no questions to answer when I would take her out.

One Sunday, I went to church, and the pastor's sermon convicted me throughout that entire service. I recall coming home, taking all her clothes off her, and laying her on the sofa. She stretched her body out and laid on the sofa in complete peace, I knew then that I had to be comfortable with her. At that moment, both of our lives changed, and it became my mission to make her the strong, fearless individual that she has become today.

She got her first prosthetic at six months and began walking at ten months; from that time, she ran everywhere. I dared her to allow others to kill the confidence that I spent years building. She would insist on pity parties, and I would insist on "suck it up!" It would have been easier to allow her to just conform to society. Still, by not allowing that, she was a high school cheerleader and gymnast, who went to college and began modeling, living in Los Angeles, working as a professional model, who even got the honor of being in The Fenty Fashion Show, which was her dream. As a mother, we don't always get it right, but we can't stop pushing.

Crystal Allen is a social media, content marketing, and communications strategist who conducts social media training, networking workshops, and teaches digital strategy. She's the Founder and Chief Executive Officer of *Xpos Your Media, LLC,* a boutique media and PR agency.

She has worked in the sales and marketing industry for over 20 years and is a nurse. A mother of four and grandmother of one, she also finds time to manage three of her children's professional acting and modeling careers. You can catch Crystal on her upcoming YouTube Channel, *Th!nk !n Your Lane*, a channel created to bridge the gap between new-aged thinking versus old-school views.

• CHAPTER 11 •

I'm Still Here

If you think you can't make it because you've experienced too much and there is no way you can do anything of substance or be a productive member of society because no one will listen to you, I'm here to tell you that you're wrong. You have a purpose, and God has a plan for you. I've experienced molestation when I was three and four years old. I've been raped at least four times by men that I knew, even losing my virginity to one of them. I've experienced infidelity and have been unfaithful. I've experienced a divorce, homelessness, and being pregnant out of wedlock.

I've been a single parent. I've been through bankruptcy, experienced depression, have considered and almost committed suicide. I've been through church hurt, and I've had folks lie on me and to me that I thought loved me. I've been the one that was whispered about, pointed at, and at times shunned. I've had family members betray me and have had a so-called family member call me everything but a child of God. I've had folks that I've helped, even giving them my last only to have them turn their backs on me when I needed them the most.

Despite everything I've been through, I'm still here. I lost my virginity against my will. I was so naïve about the lines boys would use to have sex, even in junior high school. I was a very developed 12-year-old but spent my days listening to the latest boy band or reading the latest "Right On" issue, so I could get the posters for my room. My parents didn't know until about a year later, even in that, they didn't know how to deal, so they blamed me at first. There was no counseling or therapy for me, but I was told to dress so that it wouldn't happen again.

I got pregnant in my sophomore year of college. I was in denial until it was too late to get an abortion and then attempted to perform my own abortion. I praise God I was unsuccessful, but my parents couldn't have *their* daughter, who was *doing so well in college,* be an unwed mother! What would their friends think?!? So, I ended up marrying my boyfriend at the time, but little did I know that he was allergic to work and addicted to other women. We stayed married for 18 months, and my divorce became final while

I was stationed in the United Kingdom. What a happy day for me!

Life as a single parent wasn't easy, but I had sense enough to surround my son and myself with a village that would help raise my son and help us navigate our new normal. I joined a church, rededicated my life to Christ while overseas, and returned to the states, ready to find a good church home. This time solidified my faith in God and that God could keep me, would keep me, and make sure that ALL my needs were met.

I moved to Georgia with a job transfer and for a slower lifestyle for my son. It was there that I met my current husband. He was and is a godsend to my son and me. God has a way of giving you everything you want and ALL of what you need, and He did that when my husband entered my life. Has life been easy for us? NOPE, not all the time! However, all things are possible with God, and our good days outweigh the bad. Fast forward a few years, I was offered a position in Michigan. I took it because I knew it would set my family up to be financially straight in the future. This location would be temporary for me as I had no intention of moving my family to the North's tundra.

Remember the entire previous trauma I had been through? I had never lived by myself, just me, ever. I left my parent's home to live with my aunt. I left my aunt's home to live in the college dorms and had a roommate. I left the dorms as a married woman. I left Georgia and moved back to California with a child and back at my parent's home. When I got married again, I had been a parent for eight years, so I had never just lived alone. So, I was forced to deal with ME.

This was a whole new thing that I had to work through. I had to come to terms with having time for me, just me. I didn't have to rush home to get dinner ready for my family because I was by myself in Michigan. I didn't have to do anything but go to work and come home, which was lonely for me. I realized during this time that I had never dealt with past trauma, past demons, and other issues that were now popping up because I was no longer so busy that I didn't have to deal with them.

During this time, my mental state hit rock bottom, and I was ready to end it all, seriously. I wrote a letter, making sure that my kids were going to be taken care of, and was ready to sleep my way into oblivion. During that dark time, the only thing that saved me were two ministers who went back and forth with me on Twitter and referred me to a good church in Michigan to get some good teaching and have someone love on me. They have no idea how much they saved my life. I still have the letter as a reminder that I was saved from making a permanent decision during a temporary situation. **Despite everything, I'm still here, and since you're reading this, you are too.**

Katrina Golden has added "author" to her list of accomplishments with her addition to this anthology. She is a veteran of the United States Air Force, has spent 25 years with the Civil Service, and now owns and runs her own bakery!

Katrina was raised in Fairfield, CA, and the youngest of three children born to Taylor and Renee Colquitt, has traveled worldwide, and now resides in Grovetown, GA, with her husband and three adult children. She loves helping others as she has been a foster parent in California, and now is very active in her church outreach ministry. Katrina credits her faith in God and her husband's love with everything she has accomplished thus far.

· CHAPTER 12 ·

What's Love Got to Do with It?

Our lives seemed to be going well. We were a blended family who did everything together. My two bonus daughters were living with us full-time and got along well with my two children. My husband was a hard-working, hands-on type of partner. We always involved everyone in all family activities; no one was excluded. We created a romantic environment that was non-discriminatory and whole. I was sitting on cloud nine because I knew I had hit the jackpot with my husband, children, and life in general.

He walked into the apartment as I was cooking and said he needed to talk to me. I quickly finished dinner and fixed the kids' plates. I had no idea what the topic of discussion would be; however, I knew it had to be important because he never called me into our room for a "talk." I can't remember his exact words, but I remember him saying he wanted to leave me. I was stunned. I asked him if it was someone else. Undoubtedly, he wouldn't say right away. The tears started to flow, and I was unable to move. At that moment, I knew my second marriage was on the brink of ending. I didn't know what to do. We talked for a while, and that's when it all began.

Shortly after the talk, I read his emails, text messages, listened to voice mails, recorded odometer readings, checked his wallet, and searched through his clothes. I found out it was indeed someone else, but I was hit with a ton of bricks when I discovered who. This woman was a friend of mine. I experienced a roller coaster of emotions. I felt angry, hurt, betrayed, insecure, inadequate, and depressed. I lost 40 pounds in a short amount of time and was completely lost.

I did the only thing I knew how to do, pray! I began searching the web for answers to save my marriage. I came across a lifeline in the book: *The Power of a Praying Wife* and the *Prayer and Study Guide* by Stormie Omartian. I worked diligently as I sought the Lord for answers. The answers came slowly. For the next two years, we went to counseling and separated for six months. I prayed, begged, and pleaded, but he would not stop seeing her. At one point, he thought he wanted to be with her instead of me. I was devastated.

I continued to pray for God to save my marriage. Little did I know, I was actually developing a real relationship with Him and working on me at the same time. I learned that God doesn't change people because you ask Him to, but He will change you. My husband revealed some troubling things that happened in his past, and he wanted to get better. He wanted me to work on it with him. At first, I was hesitant. After all, HE is the one who cheated. Why did I need to go to counseling? Since I wanted my marriage to work, I agreed. So, we joined a 12-step program that dealt with addictions. We did it together, as individuals and as a couple.

The recovery program was a huge factor in us reconciling. I learned a lot about myself as well as his issues. One important thing I learned is that marriage will change you, hopefully for the better. If you're not ready to examine your behaviors, attitudes, and beliefs, then you are not ready for marriage. As painful as my discovery was, it was necessary. I also learned that it was not my fault. He was responsible for his own behaviors. There was absolutely nothing I could have done to make him not stray, absolutely NOTHING. Having more sex with him, cooking more, cleaning more, losing weight - none of those things was guaranteed to keep him from cheating.

I ultimately learned that I have no control over anyone else. That reality was difficult to grasp because I lived my life trying to control every aspect of it. So, not being able to keep this from happening was tearing at my core and self-esteem. How do you trust your husband again? How do you get past the hurt and anger? Trusting in God and time? Trusting God first has worked for me. When I turn all my fears and doubts over to God and truly surrender, miracles happen. Opportunities for honest dialogue open and the healing begins.

I take it one day at a time, and I look at his behavior, not his words. If he is "acting" like the man I fell in love with, then it is a good day. My focus is no longer on where he is and what he is doing. I trust God to handle everything in this relationship. No matter how I'm feeling or when we have a disagreement, big or small, I know this too shall pass. Eventually, I will have my peace and serenity day by day. Our love and trust grew slowly, and I think everything happened in God's time. I watched for evidence of his trustworthiness. Meaning, over time, he gives me a reason to trust him. Thankfully, both of us wanted to move past it all and focus on the future – together.

What's love got to do with it? It has everything to do with it. Love takes time, dedication, willingness to change, and work. It's possible to survive infidelity if you're both willing to do the work. There are several books, websites, and groups dedicated to this very subject. Your marriage can survive, and you can become one again.

Tameka Hudson is a minister's wife, mother, entrepreneur, baker, and co-author. She is a native of Atlanta, Georgia, where she resides with her husband of 17 years, Pastor Earl Amis Hudson.

She is the co-founder of Come as You Are to Christ Ministry with her husband, owner of *Hudson's Baked Cakes, LLC,* and an athletic clothing line set to debut in Fall 2021, *Fit Black Chic and Fit Black Dude.* She graduated from Tuskegee University with a bachelor's degree and later from Central Michigan University with her master's degree. Her greatest fulfillment in life comes through baking, inspiring others to love God and themselves, and spending time with her family. Earl and Tameka are the proud parents of four adult children.

• CHAPTER 13 •

Whoosah, It's Okay

If I ever needed to rely on God's promises that I am quick to give others, I sho' need them for myself now.

"Lo, I am with you always, even unto the end of the world. Amen." - Matthew 28:20 (KJV)

"Behold, I give unto you power to tread on serpents and scorpions, and over all the power of the enemy: and nothing shall by any means hurt you." – Luke 10:19 (KJV)

"No weapon that is formed against thee shall prosper; and every tongue that shall rise against thee in judgement thou shalt condemn." – Isaiah 54:17(KJV)

"Vengeance is mine; I will repay, saith the Lord." – Romans 12:19(KJV)

After being out of the office for a few days, I walk in, and my boss says to me, "Come on Mrs. V, let's take a walk; I need to talk to you." In my mind, I am questioning, what has happened, what is going on? As we make it around the block and begin to climb the hill, my body becomes numb; tears fill my eyes and slowly begin to fall. My boss reaches for my hand and reassures me that we will get through this together. He tells me that he believes in me and reminds me that God has me! He tells me how infuriated he is and when he finds out who did this, they will be out of there.

As we continue to walk, I regain my composure; I assure my boss that I am good and okay. Wow, this is a lot, yet I promise not to say anything and treat everyone the same. As my exterior displayed constraint, poise, and strength, my inner being has crumbled within my mind. I am questioning God as to why He would allow this to happen to me; how can I live my life abundantly if my past continues to try to destroy me? I even began to remind God that it was Him that brought me here, I was fine where I was, and now He brings me here to be destroyed.

See, over 20 plus years ago, I made some terrible decisions, decisions that completely changed the course of my life. Decisions that landed me to serve time in prison, decisions that still to this day try to hunt me down with the intent to annihilate me, yes, not only to knock me off my feet but to destroy me.

The devil, the prince of the air, is very cunning, distracting, and deceitful, yet everything he does is not a secret. His story is recorded in the Holy Bible, John 10:10 – *"The thief comes only to steal and kill and destroy."* He comes to steal your identity and thoughts, kill your future dreams and present opportunities, and destroy your character! Yes, that is exactly it! If he can stop you from learning lessons from what you have experienced, he knows that you will never fulfill your destined purpose here on earth.

Sis, he almost had me. Although I said I was good, although I went back serving and helping everyone, I became depressed, bitter, my peace was taken, and I regretted coming to this place. A place I felt would catapult me to my desired goal, has now become a place of misery. No longer would I come in chipper, happy, motivated, and encouraging others. No, I didn't want to hear others' sob stories as they didn't seem to care or understand what I was dealing with. Well, the more I attempted to feed people with a long handle spoon and not allow them to emotionally nor mentally enter my space, the closer they came, and the more I found myself forgetting about my situation.

I'm open to serving others, I mean that is what God would do. As Joseph is recorded in Genesis 50:20 saying to his brothers, *"You meant evil against me, but God used it for good,"* I had to pause and laugh. Wow, that was a low blow, but I'm not going anywhere. I am not a fraud, and I am not my past. You can no longer hold this over my head; no longer will I walk in shame; it is what it is. We've all experienced some horrific things in our lives, some more challenging than others, but the key is we have overcome them all. It doesn't matter where you began or how it came to be, what matters is how it ends, and God says, *"You are more than a conqueror."*-Romans 8:37

Sis, I share my testimony with great apprehension and know that you may feel the same when you make up your mind to move forward in life, but today, the buck stops here. Today we tell the devil (that thing or person that is mentally holding us back) you have no authority over me, and you can go on with that foolery. I know who I am and whose I am! I've been bought with a price and I am a *daughter of the King!* No matter what situations you've experienced, it did not destroy you. It only shook things up and caused a slight delay.

Now, it's time for you to wake up, get up, and get moving! It's your time! You did not go through the flood without being overtaken, nor be thrown in the midst of fire and not get burned only to sit down and not flourish and thrive. Sis, you've cried long enough, and your past has been the excuse for far too long. Your *brighter day* is here, so take hold of it knowing *that "all things are working for your good."* – Romans 8:28

Hey sis, I see you, that crown adorned upon your head, you wear it well. Oh, you didn't know, every battle, obstacle, and messy situation that you've overcome represents the jewels in your crown. Yesss gurrl, straighten up that crown, and whoosah, it's okay!

Verlisa Wearing, tenderly called Elder V, is an ordained minister, founder of A Brighter Day Ministry, radio host, writer, hospitality industry executive, and Deacon Ronald Wearing's wife. She believes that in order to see change, you must focus and create change within yourself to help bring change in others.

When asked how she handles life's struggles, she states that "The sun must shine in every storm. If we just get through this, we will be stronger and wiser than ever. There will be brighter days." She believes that her greatest is accomplishment is being the mommy of David, Daylon, and Cai.

Connect with Elder V at www.abrighterday.net; Facebook.com/Verlisa.Wearing; Twitter @ElderVerlisa, and Instagram @ElderVerlisa

• CHAPTER 14 •

A Letter to My 15-year-old Self

I would ask how you are doing, but I already have a good idea. First, I want to say I love you. I know it's not easy being you right now, with the lack of support and the uncertainties you're facing. No one should ever have to endure the pain you are feeling at this moment. I worry about you as you fight this battle, constantly viewing your life with trepidation. I am writing this letter to you because I know you're scared and alone. But before I go on, please know you won! You eliminated that demon and destroyed his existence by taking back your power.

I danced and sang to one of my favorite songs in my room as I packed my preferred pink pajamas for my trip. That summer was going to be an epic prelude to high school. However, it was the most tumultuous experience a teenage girl should ever have to endure. What should have been the best summer of my life turned into the "bane of my existence." I didn't see the signs, and I know it wasn't my fault! The insurmountable pain created an insecure girl who wanted to destroy her entire being. I went to sleep each night thinking I was protected, not knowing I would wake up to a demon staring in my face with dark and venomous eyes.

I thought the new pajamas with the little ballerinas would protect me. They were my favorite, and I felt adorable. They were not too childish, but they weren't sexy, either. I wasn't ready for the crop top t-shirt and boy shorts. They were comfortable and warm enough for those possible frigid nights. The cuteness faded along with the innocence when they were torn off weeks later and lay strewn across the room. I remember feeling like I was being dragged into a dark sewer, and my flesh was being ripped from my frail body with every touch of the calloused fingers and jagged fingernails that rubbed across my skin.

There was a horrible smell. It was a putrid combination of hot, rotting, musk, and pure evil. An even more powerful scent engulfed the room while I gasped for breath. It was fear like I had never experienced in my life. Something terrible was happening that I knew wasn't beautiful. This was ugly, painful and unwanted. It was wrong! Months went by, and I found myself staring at the ceiling and then my wrist, something I often did. This particular morning, I noticed how prominent my veins were as I ran the razor up and down my arm, across and zig zag. They were a mixture of dark green, purple, and blue. The razor made a few nicks and a couple of small gashes on my wrist, but I just couldn't figure out the right vein.

I didn't want more pain; I just wanted the existing pain to go away. While I was planning my debut with the Mississippi Bridge, my classmates were excited about dancing the night away in their frilly dresses with their dates. That night I gazed at the bridge that seemed larger than life. This was supposed to be the night I ended it all, but I was too scared. Dammit, how the hell are you supposed to climb onto that bridge when you are afraid of heights? I couldn't. I didn't.

Many years later, I heard a voice that told me that I needed to learn how to survive amid emotional turbulence. I couldn't face the person in the mirror, so I became a shell with a mask. Not the kind that Superheroes don. I was a newly created, well-made-up woman with repressed feelings, easily triggered by touch, smell, or a glance from someone. I was weary from fighting the demons of the past and tired from pretending to be happy. My body had grown numb and weak…

However, the mask will have to be removed to heal that battered spirit. You will finally realize you can no longer live your life as an imposter beautifully adorned with a fake image. The people in your life have a right to know your real identity, including you. One day you will ask God to kill the beast or make it invisible. He will give you his word, and you will experience the power in His promise years later. As you start to peel away the mask bit by bit, it will reveal some ugly "ish." Through that pain will be a discovery of strength and a light that shines big as the diamond you are.

You believe this tragedy has made you unworthy of love. You are afraid people will see through that stone wall, and your cover will be blown. Baby girl, you will meet an amazing man who will love you with every inch of his soul. He will protect you and reignite your spirit! You will have two beautiful and talented daughters who will love you immensely. You will have friends, and there will be one who will have a tremendous impact on you. You will be so unapologetically phenomenal! You'll look in a mirror and take your own breath away!

I could go on forever because I have so much more to share, but there are many lessons you will have to learn. The rape happened, but it is not your existence, and it did not destroy you. The attempts to end your life didn't happen because God had a better plan. He kept His word and made him invisible. Are you finally healed? Hell no, but you will get there with time. You won't be free from the tragedy, but the memory will not consume you. Although the mask has been removed, it will hang in your crevice heart as a reminder to protect your spirit and never give your power to another broken soul!

With all my love
Me

Elicia Moore has a heart of gold and a fierce enthusiasm for life. As a writer, she hopes to reach other women who have challenges they are struggling to overcome. Elicia lives in Georgia with her husband and has two amazing daughters.

As a former dancer, she relishes the art of looking her best and staying fit. While studying to be a wellness and fitness coach, she inspires and encourages women of all ages to live their best lives. Although she has had significant challenges in her life, it has never stopped her from achieving greatness. She is confident and bold. Her daily mantra is, "I am unapologetically grateful for this life that God has gifted me."

CHAPTER 15

Please Don't Judge Me

Dear Black Women,

I am writing this to you because it bothers me that we continue to hurt and judge each other. Some of my greatest hurts and disappointments have been done by you. We continuously complain about how we are mistreated by the men we love. But we hurt and judge each other every day. Every time I try to bond and connect with you, it ends in rejection.

One Friday night, I decided to join two of my friends and some of their friends for dinner and drinks. It was a table full of beautiful black women chatting and chewing. In the middle of the ongoing chatter and laughter, one of my friend's coworkers asked me, "You do not have **any** children? What's wrong with you? Why don't you have any children?" Everyone got silent and looked at me. This was supposed to be a chill moment for me. I was supposed to feel comfortable and happy as I sat there, drinking margaritas and having some dinner with the girls. But now I sat there with a judge and jury. I felt exposed and paralyzed by her judgmental words.

Her words instantly unraveled my confidence. It became a defining moment in my views about myself. What **was** wrong with me? Why was I still not married and not a mother? Even though I looked like the other women who sat around that table, I had been singled out as the only one there who **did not** have children. It became a painful moment for me. It was not supposed to be like this. I was supposed to feel safe, confident, and secure with other black women, but they were all staring and judging me.

The woman who asked me the inappropriate question (or the judge) had always been friendly to me in the past. Maybe I had said something that made her think that it was ok to judge me and question my mere existence as a Black woman. I am not sure what my answer was because I was so devastated by the question. She (my accuser) was a single mother. Even though she was correct that I did not have any children, she did not know that I had devoted myself to being the village to women like her. At work and outside of work, I helped youth in the community and helped single mothers with their kids.

As I thought back on that day and other similar moments, I realized that this was common for us. Black women judge each other for everything! We judge our looks (hair, clothes, etc.), our status (single, married, no children, etc.), and we also judge our skin color (dark skin vs. light skin). Black women should not judge each other but should try to stick together because we are already judged by everyone else. We are scrutinized in the workplace by men and other women of color. We must understand that when we continue to judge each other that it diminishes our power and presence.

My experience at the Friday night dinner with my friend's co-worker had a damaging effect, and I began to avoid hanging out with women in those types of settings. It took me a while to heal from the hurt and the scrutiny. Eventually, I realized that this one episode did not define my worth. We are some of the most beautiful people in all shapes, colors, and sizes, but we always show our ugly to each other. Black women are stronger when we stick together. Every day we fight against each other at work and play. Why can't we try to understand and respect our differences? We should identify our common ground and so that we can become stronger together. Why should we stick together?

- **We give and share the strongest love (but refuse to extend our love to each other and give men all our love)**

- **We always forgive so many others (but we continue to judge each other and hold past experiences against each other).**

I hope you will consider everything that I said to love and support each other. I will fight like a girl against this forever! I will continue to compliment other black women (even the ones that I do not know.)

Edwina is a purpose-driven writer from Georgia who is motivated by the beauty and pain of her experiences. She writes to inspire, help and educate others. She is in love with coffee, storytelling, and passionate about family and community.

· CHAPTER 16 ·

Changing My Focus from Man to God

As Deborah Cox plays …

How did you get here?
I've spent all my life, on a search to find
The love who'll stay for eternity
The heaven-sent to fulfill my needs
But when I turn around
Again, love has knocked me down…

This was the last in a string of relationships leading to nowhere. I knew if I told my mother about the pregnancy, I would keep the baby. This was not how I imagined my life. Where did I go wrong? Reflecting over my past, what could I have done differently? I could do nothing but fall on my knees and cry out, "Why did you leave me?" My father died when I was only six years old. Each celebration, accomplishment, and failure was accompanied by sadness. Who would heal my heart? Who was going to hold me tight when I had nightmares? Who was going to show me how a man should treat a woman?

Although I heard how much he loved me, I stilled wanted, no needed him. The squeaky sound from him walking down the stairs stopped my tears. "Oh no," I said; he must have heard me crying. I quickly wiped the remaining tears from my eyes as he placed his arms around me and said, "Things will get better, I promise." This brings me little comfort, and we just continued with the day as nothing had happened.

Being an *analytical* person, I began to trace every relationship to see what contributed to me being where I thought I would never be. I had bought into the American Dream. Looking over each stage of my life, I started to understand how my past unhealed trauma was controlling my decisions. Although I understood more about my journey, I was still trying to create a perfect family. The more controlling I became; the more frustrated people were with me. It's too much! I can't handle it! Nothing was getting better; instead, things were getting worse.

Deborah Cox was playing in the back of my head, "How did he get here?" In the words of Dr. Phil, "You must rise above your raising." I had done that, or so I thought. I was a professional in Corporate America, making a good salary with benefits. Why wasn't this enough? I was amid an avalanche, and everything around me was coming down. This is not the person I set out to be. Everyone who had bought into the "independent woman" facade was just as confused.

The consequences of my choices were beginning to show. Is this how an addict feels when they hit rock bottom? What was my addiction? I didn't do drugs! I wasn't promiscuous! I didn't smoke, not even cigarettes! I had to go deeper. I had to get to the root of my problem. What caused me to be with this man I knew not quite long but had given so much? The same intensity of my pain craved the same intensity of passion.

The stress had taken a toll on me. I was having chest pain, shortness of breath, headaches, and snapping at my children. I was referred to a cardiologist to see if I had heart problems, especially since I was diagnosed as a child with Mitral Valve Prolapse. The doctor informed me that if I did not manage my stress, I would eventually be placed on medication, need a valve repair, or heart transplant, if not suffer a sudden heart attack. When she walked out of the room, I looked up to the sky and said, "What am I supposed to do? Is it to abandon my mother, quit my job, give away my kids, and divorce my husband?"

I was referred to a psychiatrist, where I was initially diagnosed with anxiety and severe depression. I have arrived at this point of brokenness due to a multitude of trials. My life was spiraling out of control after dealing with my brother's death, my mother's disability, my daughter's health challenges, marital problems, personal health issues, and employment discrimination. Although I was saved around 12, it wasn't until 35 when God became the Lord of my life. Things got to a point where I could no longer cope. I realized that I could not do it alone.

Although I had tried to fill the void in my life with my accomplishments, it didn't work. I found myself in church crying, unconcerned about who was looking at me, or what they were thinking. I just wanted to be saved from the pain of loneliness, childhood wounds, and from the ridicule of being different! Each time I went to church, I experienced a greater level of satisfaction. I learned that God loved me just as I was, and I didn't have to be ashamed of the mistakes I had made. Each time I heard a sermon, it felt as though the pastor knew what I was going through. A sense of satisfaction overcame me like never before. It was the kind of high that every addict chased, and saved people felt.

The emptiness inside was being filled with unconditional love. All that was expected of me was to accept that Jesus was the son of God, believe that He had forgiven me for my sins, and repent. My path, although backward, is becoming clearer and clearer, and somehow feels like things are falling into place. Now when I face a hurdle, the words to Kirk Franklin, "Lean on Me," play in my head. I know that whatever happens, God will work everything out for the good of those who believe in Him. I have replaced my fear of abandonment, rejection, and neglect with the understanding that God will always love me, and I am never alone. Instead of operating from a false-strength position (pride); I now operate out of God's strength (faith). I focus on fellowshipping with other believers, breaking generational curses, and communicating consequences with grace and dignity.

NICOLE JONES

Native Atlantian and UGA graduate with BS Statistics; Rose Calloway began her 25+ career as an analyst. She provided kinship care for members of her family, including becoming an adoptive parent.

Supporting the children in her family led to volunteering at Elizabeth Baptist Church's youth department and becoming a member of disability organizations throughout the United States of America. She turned her education, work, and volunteer experience into a position with Atlanta Public Schools, P2P of Georgia, Morehouse School of Medicine and now a contractor.

While getting the children help, she recognized her own disability. She uses her experiences to help families with children in crisis. Her one-to-one coaching empowers parents to advocate for their children. She believes that consulting with organizations can provide a family-centered perspective to address the social determinants of health. She is passionate about helping those who want help, but lack the means or ability to obtain the appropriate resources.

CHAPTER 17

Second Wind, My Story Is Changing

RESTORATION:
JEREMIAH 33:6-7, 11
But now take another look. I'm going to give this city a thorough renovation, working a true healing inside and out. I'm going to show them life whole, life brimming with blessings. (7) I'll restore everything that was lost to Judah and Jerusalem, I'll build everything back as good as new. (11) I'll restore everything that was lost in the land, I'll make everything as good as new. "I God, Says So"

I'm reminded of when my family and I became homeless in November 2017. It was literally the day after Thanksgiving. I was completely devastated, embarrassed, and most of all, I felt like a failure to my three children. Although my husband and I were both working full-time jobs, life still happened. While putting two children through college and amongst other things, "LIFE HAPPENED!"

We lost our apartment thirty days before my daughter was scheduled to walk across the stage from Michigan State University with a Bachelor of Arts, majoring in Sociology. We put our happy faces on, but no one in my family knew what was going on, nor the things my husband and I were facing. My best friend, who I love dearly and will always be grateful for, allowed my husband, our youngest son, and I to stay in one of her bedrooms since her children were away at college as well. The three of us packed in the one room and slept on an air mattress.

We continued to get up every morning to go to work. I made sure that my son continued to go to school every day. Yet, I cried out asking God, "Why us, why does this have to happen to me?" Despite all of what we were going through, my husband and I continued to go to church and serve our Pastor, the late Dr. Rev. Archie Matlock Sr. We paid our tithes on time, and our children finished the school year strong. Our faith never wavered, and we believed that God would somehow bring us through.

I had never faced anything like this before. Some days I felt as if I were losing my mind. It was hard, but I never lost my faith in God. I had to stand on the same faith that I often shared with others. I heard God speak to me and say that He would give me a "Second Wind!" My God! Ninety-six days later, God allowed me and my husband to start completely over, Thank you, Jehovah. God provided us with the resources to move into a new apartment. We were so blessed that the new landlord did not ask to do a credit check. The only requirement was to have income and two years of employment. Thank God my husband and I had over five years of employment at the same job. God restored it all, and in some areas, we received a double portion!

While we were going through, I would read Jeremiah 33 every night as I held on to God's word and His promise. In the process, not only did God tell me that He would bring my family and me out, but He wanted me to go back and help other families. He instructed me to share my testimony without shame. He wanted me to tell it with the boldness of His faithfulness. It was this boldness that led me to birth my first non-profit organization, *"Cora's Helping Hands Inc,"* where I serve families of all nationalities across the state of Illinois who are facing homelessness or coming out of a similar situation. Cora's Helping Hands helps families to recover and restore their lives by meeting their individual needs.

I wrote this story to encourage someone that no matter where you may be in your life right now, there is power in your testimony, and your testimony is definitely to help someone else. Sometimes you have to share what you have learned and what you may be going through, even amid the process. Your progress is a testimony that God is working, and your story is changing. Trust the process.

You are an overcomer! Share from a place where you have been healed, and if you are not there yet, don't be afraid to share it anyway. Someone needs your story. Show others that you are proof that God can do it! Show them there is still hope and that you are the evidence. Don't be afraid of where you come from because "YOU HAVE COME FROM IT!"

Say this prayer:
Father God, I just want to say thank you for keeping my family and me amid all uncertain times. Thank You for never taking your hands of protection away.

Thank You for the restoration! Father God, I ask that whoever may read this and maybe facing any difficulties right now, that you send them clarity on their next decision and guide them. Let them know that whatever was lost, you are the God that can restore and allow their testimony to be a drawing agent to share with others about your love.

Father God blow on them and give them a "Second Wind" and allow their stories to continue to change their lives for your glory, in Jesus' name, amen.

Shanta Hogan Walker is a walking, talking, modern-day miracle who knows firsthand what a second wind can do to someone's life trajectory.

Shanta is intentional about giving God the glory for overcoming the obstacles and odds of being homeless with her family for ninety-six days. She serves her community and family by teaching others with faith-based principles on love, hope, and charity, enacting change everywhere she goes.

A native of Chicago's West Side neighborhoods, Shanta saw firsthand what struggling communities looked like and their people. Married to her devoted husband, Jessie Walker, this selfless mother of three, Tynaya, Derrick, and Kamren, has a heart for communities and their families. Shanta's mission to help people has grown into a budding 501c (3) called ***Cora's Helping Hands Inc,*** ® where she is the founder and CEO of this non-profit organization. Shanta is on a mission to help millions of families across the Midwest.

Made in the USA
Monee, IL
17 April 2021